Decorative Painting on
Glass, Ceramics
and Metal

To my husband John for his constant support,
my daughters Rebecca and Ruth for keeping me young
and my mother-in-law Doreen for keeping us all organised.

Decorative Painting on
Glass, Ceramics and Metal

JUDY BALCHIN

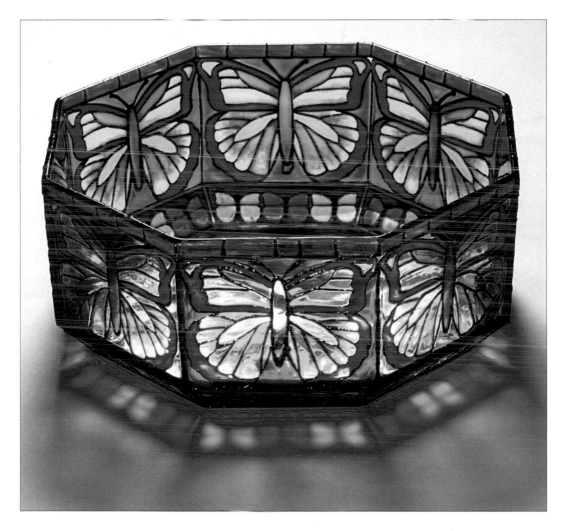

SEARCH PRESS

First published in Great Britain 1998

Search Press Limited
Wellwood, North Farm Road,
Tunbridge Wells, Kent TN2 3DR

Text copyright © Judy Balchin

Photographs by Search Press Studios
Photographs and design copyright © Search Press Ltd. 1998

ISBN 0 85532 838 X

Suppliers

If you have any difficulty in obtaining any of the materials and equipment mentioned in this book, then please write to the publishers for a current list of stockists, which includes firms who operate a mail-order service:

Search Press Limited, Wellwood,
North Farm Road, Tunbridge Wells,
Kent TN2 3DR, England

Colour separation by P&W Graphics, Singapore
Printed in Spain by Elkar S. Coop. Bilbao 48012

I would like to give special thanks to John Wright of Pebeo UK Ltd., Unit 109, Solent Business Centre, Millbrook, Southampton, SO15 0HW for supplying the majority of the paints used in this book; ColArt, Whitefriars Avenue, Wealdstone, Harrow, Middlesex, HA3 5RH for contributing paints; Fenwick Limited, Royal Victoria Place, Tunbridge Wells, Kent, TN1 2SR for providing the props for photography; and Lowenna McGrellis for taking the photograph of me that appears at the front of this book.

Special thanks are also due to the friendly team at Search Press who made working on this book such fun – in particular, Commissioning Editor Roz Dace for her support and encouragement, Editor Chantal Porter for her dedication and help, Julie Wood for her design skills, and Lotti de la Bédoyère for her photography.

I would also like to thank all the students who have attended my workshops. They have been so enthusiastic that it has been a pleasure teaching them.

PAGE 1
Green wine bottle

This is decorated using the freestyle one-stroke technique (see pages 50–51). Non-waterbased ceramic paints have been used to give an opaque coverage.

Small decanter

This is painted with non-waterbased glass paints. Whilst still wet, non-waterbased ceramic paints are dropped on, and allowed to dribble.

Small green bottle

This green bottle is decorated with gold waterbased porcelain paint. Small squares of masking tape are applied to the neck and lower half of the bottle. The base of the neck and the middle of the bottle are then masked with strips of tape. The neck and lower half of the bottle are sponged with gold paint and the masking tape is removed immediately.

PAGE 3
Butterfly bowl

This beautiful glass bowl is decorated using non-waterbased glass paints and black outliner. For more details about this bowl, turn to page 44.

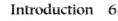

Contents

Introduction

Painted and decorated china, glass and metalware have always fascinated me. I love visiting antique and junk shops. There, I can absorb the wonderful patterns and images created by craftsmen and women throughout the years. This has, however, been quite a frustrating pastime . . . until recently. I had often wondered how I could reproduce that professional finish without the aid of a kiln, and without the knowledge of the different glazes used for decoration. Then, to my delight, I discovered a whole range of paints that could be applied to china, glass and metal which did not require firing in a kiln. These paints can be applied to any smooth surface, they are durable and give a truly professional finish. This discovery has opened up a whole new exciting world for me, my students and fellow craft enthusiasts. We can now create our own designs, and paint items to match existing surroundings and decor. I still browse around antique and junk shops, but I also visit charity and kitchen shops, hunting for inexpensive and original pieces to paint. I seek objects with pleasing or unusual shapes which could be enhanced by decoration.

Glass festive plate
(see pages 40–43)

Ceramic cat mug
(see page 26)

This book has taken me on an exciting journey; I have experimented with the paints and discovered many different techniques, all of which I now share with you in these pages. Whilst writing this book I have, at times, felt as though I have been working in an antique shop! Many nights have been spent engrossed in my work, surrounded by plates, cups, vases, bottles and other treasures. It has been exciting and satisfying to gradually transform these pieces into beautiful and unique objects, vibrant with colour and rich in texture.

Having worked in the design world for over twenty years, a plain vase or plate holds no fears for me. I just cannot wait to pick up my paintbrush and start work. However, I can understand a beginner feeling a little daunted by the thought of drawing or painting a design on to a blank item. In my workshops I constantly hear my students saying 'I cannot draw – I could not possibly do that!' However, you do not necessarily need to be able to draw expertly. Inspiration can be found in many different places: wallpaper, greetings cards, fabric, packaging, wrapping paper and magazines are all useful starting points for designs. Keep your eyes open for unusual colour combinations and patterns. Just a tiny snippet from one of these could inspire you. Try to record any ideas in a scrapbook. A camera is also a good way of recording design ideas as you can photograph colours, textures and shapes in architecture and nature – church windows, flowers, foliage, trees and animals, for example. Design source books are also available; these provide an endless supply of ideas for decorative work. Patterns have been provided for all the designs in this book but once you have mastered the basic techniques, you will discover the joys of creating your own personalised designs.

Pieces can be painted to match your decor, personalised to provide a perfect gift, or simply decorated for fun. My main hope in writing this book is that you can share in the sheer pleasure I have experienced in creating something unique.

*Metal daisy bucket
(see page 71)*

Materials

All the materials and equipment used in this book are readily available from art and craft suppliers, DIY stores, stationers and supermarkets, and you may even already have many of the items in your own home. As you work with the paints you will find yourself inventing new uses for ordinary everyday materials such as absorbent paper, cotton buds, cocktail sticks and sponges – these can all be put to good use. A comprehensive list of all the materials and equipment needed for every project featured in this book is provided on page 12.

Keep your eyes open for items to decorate. Junk shops and charity shops provide a rich source, along with kitchen, homeware and DIY outlets. Odd cups, saucers and teapots can be painted with the same decoration to form a new, coordinated tea set (see page 55). So, search those kitchen cupboards, collect old bottles and jars (especially ones with unusual shapes) and do not throw anything away!

Paints

All the paints used in this book are specially designed to adhere to smooth surfaces. There are no hard and fast rules about using particular paints for particular projects, but they each have different qualities and some are more suitable for certain techniques. I always look for durability as well as a professional finish. What could be more disappointing than to complete a project only to discover a few weeks later that the paint has begun to chip, or wash off. Ceramic items that come into contact with food need to be particularly durable, so I use the waterbased porcelain paints that are baked in the oven. Ornamental items however, can be decorated using any of the paints. Glass pieces cry out for translucent glass paints and metal items for a more opaque coverage. As you become familiar with the paints, the decision as to which type to use will become more obvious.

1. *Non-waterbased ceramic paints*

2. *Waterbased porcelain paint outliners*

3. *Waterbased porcelain paints*

4. *Waterbased acrylic paints*

5. *Non-waterbased glass paints*

6. *Glass painting outliners*

Waterbased porcelain paints

These paints are available in transparent, semi-transparent and opaque ranges and in a variety of colours which are intermixable. Decorated items must be baked in a domestic oven to make them durable. The paints can be applied thinly to reveal brushstrokes, or thickly for a more opaque finish. They are touch dry within half an hour, which is a great advantage when painting a multi-coloured piece. A smaller range of colours and metallic finishes are available in outliner form. These are squeezed from a tube to provide a fine outline which is useful for more detailed work.

Painted pieces should be left to air-dry for twenty-four hours, or longer if the paint has been applied thickly. Baking hardens the glaze and produces a highly professional finish. Set the temperature of the oven to 150–160°C (300–325°F or gas mark 2–3). Place your item in the cold oven and then allow it to slowly heat up – this prevents fragile pieces from cracking. When the oven reaches the required temperature, bake for thirty-five minutes. It is a good idea to bake a test piece first on an old tile as oven temperatures vary slightly.

Waterbased acrylic paints

These air-drying paints are available in a large range of colours and in a gloss, matt or pearl finish. They produce an excellent flat finish (see the terracotta pots on pages 56–61) and dry quickly between coats. If used on metal or ceramicware the finished piece should be given a coat of clear varnish for added protection. Items can be cleaned in warm soapy water and polished dry.

These flowers are outlined using black outliner and then filled in with waterbased porcelain paints.

Waterbased porcelain paints are applied using large, random brush strokes.

Waterbased acrylic paints are used to paint flowers on to a yellow base. They are then outlined with a brush and randomly sponged.

Non-waterbased ceramic paints

These air-drying paints are available in a good range of colours. They are intermixable and are excellent for opaque coverage. Brushes should be cleaned in white spirit. Beautiful dribbling and splattering effects can be created using these paints (see pages 21 and 72–76). Outliners are not available in this range, but for finer detailing, paint can be decanted into a small plastic bottle fitted with a 0.5mm metal nozzle. The paint can then be piped on to the surface. The drying time for these paints is considerably longer than for waterbased paints. Paints are touch dry within four hours and completely dry in twenty-four hours. The durability of this paint is good, but added protection can be given with a coat of clear varnish. Clean your finished piece by washing in warm soapy water, then polish dry.

Non-waterbased ceramic paint is sponged on to the surface and whilst still wet it is oversponged with white spirit which is allowed to dribble.

Random brush strokes are applied using a 1cm (½in) decorative wash brush and non-waterbased ceramic paint.

Spirals of black and gold are applied using non-waterbased ceramic paint. When dry, freestyle decorative flowers are added.

Non-waterbased glass paints

These air-drying transparent paints are available in a good range of colours and are intermixable. Clear gloss glass painting varnish can be added to the paints to dilute the colours and create a more pastel range. Brushes should be cleaned in white spirit. Tubes of outliner are available in black, imitation lead, gold, silver and copper. You can use these paints for the dribbling technique (see pages 72–73). Paints are touch dry within two hours and completely dry in eight hours. You can protect your finished pieces with a coat of clear gloss glass painting varnish. Clean your finished piece by washing in cold water, then polish dry. Items painted with glass paints are purely decorative and are not suitable for everyday use.

Blue and green non-waterbased glass paints are sponged on to the vase and allowed to dry. The surface is then decorated with glass droplets, and embellished with sun rays and swirls using the imitation lead outliner.

The design is drawn on with black outliner. When dry, it is filled in using non-waterbased glass paints diluted with clear gloss glass painting varnish to create a pastel finish.

The spiral is outlined, painted with non-waterbased glass paints, then decorated with glass droplets and metallic outliners. The remaining areas are sponged and embellished with outlined gold stars.

11

Other equipment and materials

You do not need all the items featured here to begin decorative painting. A list of the equipment and materials required accompanies each project, so check this carefully before you begin.

1. **Blanks** Plain ceramic, glass and enamel pieces are readily available.

2. **Lighter fuel** This can be used to remove glue, labels and traces of grease from items before decorating. Methylated spirit may also be used.

3. **White spirit** This is used for cleaning brushes used with non-waterbased paints. It is also sponged over wet non-waterbased paints for the dribbling and splattering technique (see pages 21, 72–73).

4. **Varnish** Items painted with waterbased acrylic paints, non-waterbased ceramic paints and glass paints can be given a coat of clear varnish to protect the surface decoration.

5. **Palette** You can use a plastic palette, but a white ceramic plate covered with plastic wrap provides a cheap alternative. Simply throw away the wrap when you have finished painting.

6. **Masking tape** This is used for masking off areas that you want to remain unpainted.

7. **Pieces of sponge** Sponge can be used to apply paint. Buy a large, inexpensive one and tear off small pieces as needed.

8. **Cooling rack** This is used for drying finished painted items on.

9. **Cotton buds** Mistakes and dribbles can be removed with these.

10. **Scissors** Graphite, carbon and tracing papers can be cut to size with scissors.

11. **String** This is used to measure the rim of a pot and to help position designs (see page 58).

12. **Brushes** The projects use Nos. 2, 4 and 6 paintbrushes, a 1cm (½in) flat brush and a No. 6 rigger brush. Always look after your brushes carefully – they are the tools of your trade and should be cherished. Wash them in water or white spirit, depending on the type of paint used.

13. **Pencils** You can draw directly on to surfaces with a soft pencil (4B). A hard pencil (H) can be used when tracing a design with carbon or graphite paper.

14. **Ballpoint pen** This can be used instead of a hard pencil to transfer a design when using carbon or graphite paper.

15. **Fine waterbased felt-tip pen** Designs can be drawn directly on to the surface using this.

16. **Scalpel** Use a sharp scalpel or craft knife to cut out a stencil from stencil paper (see page 73).

17. **Cocktail sticks** These are used to scratch away areas of paint (see page 30).

18. **Tracing paper** This is used to trace your designs from the patterns in the book.

19. **Carbon paper** A transfer paper which will produce a definite and durable line to work to. It is useful when transferring designs on to glass if outliner is to cover the carbon line.

20. **Graphite paper** This is a transfer paper which will produce a soft guideline to work to. It is particularly useful when painting a pale-coloured object, as this softer line will not show through the paint.

21. **Stamps** Foam stamps mounted on to wood or clear plastic blocks are ideal for stamping on to smooth surfaces. Clear plastic blocks make it easier to position the stamp correctly.

22. **Stencil paper** This is available in different thicknesses. The finer the gauge of paper, the easier it is to cut. Acetate can also be used.

23. **Fine sandpaper** Metal items will require sanding before painting to remove any rust or uneven spots.

24. **Absorbent paper** This is an absolute necessity and is used for mopping up spillages or wiping away mistakes.

Using colour

The paints used in this book are available in a huge range of colours. However, by using just the primary colours– red, blue and yellow – you can produce a good basic range. The colour wheels on these pages provide you with a guide to refer to when deciding on your own colour combinations. The primary colours on each wheel are indicated by the small dots within the inner wheel.

Waterbased porcelain paints

These paints are baked in a domestic oven to make them more durable. The outer wheel shows how a flat vibrant range can be produced if the paints are applied generously. The inner wheel shows that, when applied thinly, brushstrokes are revealed and a more pastel range is obtained; this use of the paint is particularly effective for the one-stroke flowers and leaves (see pages 18 and 50–51).

When baking the paints, timing and temperature are extremely important (see page 9). Underbaking will reduce the durability; overbaking will dull the colours.

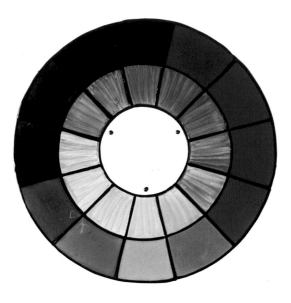

USING WATERBASED OUTLINERS

The outliners provided in this range can be used in conjunction with the paint or on their own as shown here. The metallic outliners are particularly effective when piped over a prepainted surface as fine detailing (see page 65).

Non-waterbased ceramic paints

These paints are air-dried rather than baked in a domestic oven. The outer wheel shows the range of colours that can be produced by mixing the three primary colours. The inner wheel shows the pastel range that can be achieved by adding white paint.

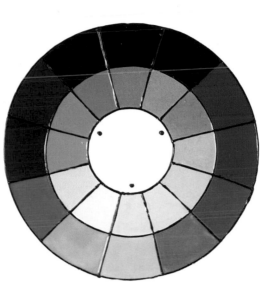

Non-waterbased glass paints

Glass paints are air-drying and have to be applied generously to obtain a flat, stained-glass effect. Sometimes, the paints may appear a little dense. The outer wheel shows the paint applied straight from the bottle, the inner wheel shows the colours achieved by adding clear gloss glass painting varnish; this lightens the density of the paint without reducing the viscosity. If you dilute the paints with white spirit, they will become thinner and brushstrokes will become visible.

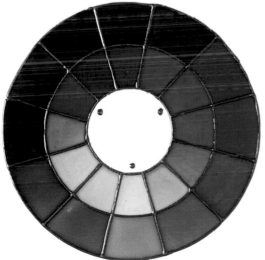

USING NON-WATERBASED OUTLINERS

There are no outliners in the non-waterbased ceramic paint range, so if you want to outline, you can decant the paint into a small plastic bottle fitted with a 0.5mm metal nozzle. Alternatively, use glass painting outliners. Black and imitation lead glass painting outliners are used to outline the basic design. It is best to apply the metallic outliners as decoration on top of a finished painted piece (see page 42), as the paints colour the lines. Outliners are ideal for lettering projects and can also be used to decorate wood, papier mâché and card.

Surfaces

These before and after photographs show clearly how plain pieces can be beautifully transformed using the right paints and a little imagination. All the techniques shown opposite are covered in the projects in this book. The techniques are simple, but it is important to prepare surfaces correctly before you start to paint. Items should be completely grease-free in order for the paint to adhere to a smooth surface.

Use a soft cloth and lighter fuel or methylated spirit to wipe over glass and ceramicware. Old metalware should be rubbed down with fine sandpaper to remove any rust spots or irregularities, then wiped down as described above to remove all debris and traces of grease. New metalware should be sanded down lightly and then wiped down. Terracotta pots should be scrubbed clean in soapy water, then dried thoroughly before decorating.

Terracotta pots, glass bottles and bowls, ceramic vases, tiles and cups, and metal goblets and bottles can all be decorated with the paints shown in this book. Here, the items have been stencilled, freepainted, finely detailed, dribbled, outlined, sponged and embellished with beads. The techniques are simple – all you need are the paints, the materials and a little imagination.

The blank items opposite were found in kitchen shops, DIY shops, garden centres and junk shops. The same items are shown above, fully decorated.

Decorative effects

Many of the techniques described in this section are used in the projects. There is no limit to the wonderful finishes you can achieve with a few paints and some simple tools. Do not be frightened to experiment. Sponging, stamping, dribbling and masking all are great fun and you will certainly create some interesting effects.

Waterbased porcelain paints

All the effects shown on these two pages have been created using waterbased porcelain paints that have been baked in an oven. It is possible to create similar effects using waterbased acrylic paints or non-waterbased ceramic or glass paints.

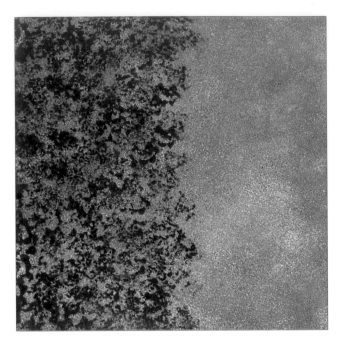

Sponging   *The background is sponged with a fine sponge using light blue paint. Darker blue is worked over the base coat using a coarser sponge to create texture.*

Using random brushstrokes   *Transparent blue paint is applied randomly and quickly to the base using a 1cm (½in) flat paintbrush. When dry, transparent yellow paint is applied on top.*

Freestyle one-stroke painting   *The flower petals and leaves are painted in one at a time using blue and green transparent paint. The stems are added with one stroke of a rigger brush.*

Outlining The designs shown at the top are outlined using coloured outliners, and the bird panel below is created using copper paint decanted into a plastic bottle fitted with a 0.5mm metal nozzle.

Stencilling The background is sponged with opaque violet. When dry, the butterfly stencil design is sponged on using a selection of darker colours.

Stamping A double row of small squares is stamped around the border using blue paint and a small square stamp. The centre is stamped with a blue daisy. The orange detailing is painted on.

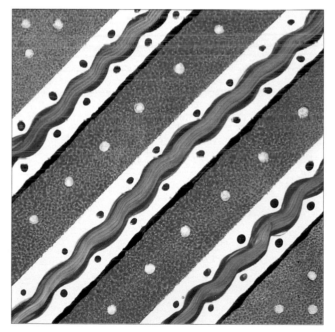

Masking Strips of masking tape are applied then the unmasked areas are sponged blue. White dots are wiped out with a cotton bud whilst the paint is still wet. The masking tape is removed and the purple lines and dots are added with a paintbrush.

Non-waterbased paints

The effects shown on these two pages are created using non-waterbased glass and ceramic paints. You can clearly see the difference between the transparent glass paints and the more opaque ceramic paints.

On this page, glass surfaces are used to demonstrate the techniques of sponging, outlining and embellishing using metallic outliners and glass beads. The designs on the page opposite are worked on a white ceramic base and introduce you to dribbling and splattering techniques. These opaque paints are ideal for folk art where vibrant flat colours are required (see pages 47 and 70).

Mottled sponging *This glass surface is sponged using two contrasting colours and a fine sponge.*

Embellishing *The surface is randomly sponged with blue and green. When dry, the heart is outlined and filled in with metallic outliner. The central glass droplet is pressed into the outliner whilst it is still wet, and small beads are embedded around the edge.*

Outlining and painting *The design is laid under the glass and is then outlined with black outliner. When dry, it is painted. Finally metallic outliners are used to add more detail.*

Creating an opaque finish *A large flat brush is used to apply a generous coat of paint. The brushstrokes are applied in the same direction to achieve a flat finish.*

Blending colours *Bands of darker and lighter blues are overlapped using a large flat brush. They are then blended together.*

Dribbling *The background is randomly sponged with blues and greens. Whilst still wet, it is lightly oversponged with white spirit and tilted so that the paints run down the surface.*

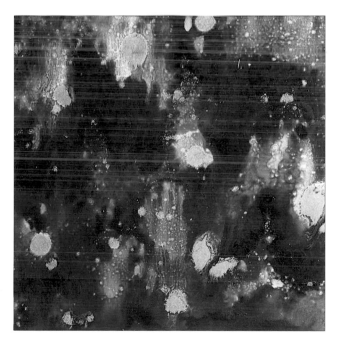

Splattering *The background is randomly sponged with turquoise and dark blue. Whilst still wet, it is oversponged with white spirit. A toothbrush is used to flick and splatter gold paint on to the surface.*

Tulip mug

SPONGING, STAMPING AND PAINTING

Sponging and stamping are the quickest and easiest ways of decorating china, yet the results are very professional. With a stamp, a few paints and some sponge, you can transform a plain mug into something special. Who knows, after completing this project, perhaps you will be inspired to stamp a complete set of mugs for your family.

YOU WILL NEED
White ceramic mug
Waterbased porcelain paints:
dark green, light green, scarlet
and yellow
3 pieces of coarse sponge
Masking tape
Tulip flower stamp
Stem and leaf stamp
1cm (½in) flat brush
No. 6 paintbrush
Palette

1. Mask the base of the handle with masking tape. Transfer your paints to the palette. Form a piece of sponge into a pad, tucking in all hard edges. Sponge the bottom third of the mug with dark green paint. Allow to dry.

2. Use a clean piece of sponge to oversponge the dark green with light green. Go over the edge slightly so that the light green shows above the dark green band. Allow to dry.

3. Paint the stem and leaf stamp with dark green paint using a No. 6 paintbrush.

4. Stamp stems and leaves evenly around the mug so that the bottom of each stem rests on the light green sponging. Allow to dry.

5. Paint the tulip flower stamp with scarlet. Stamp a tulip flower at the top of each stem. Allow to dry. Overstamp each flower with scarlet to strengthen the colour. Allow to dry.

6. Use a clean piece of sponge and yellow paint to sponge the rim of the mug and the areas in between the flowers. Allow to dry.

7. Remove the masking tape from the handle. Use a 1cm (½in) flat brush to paint the handle yellow. Leave to dry for twenty-four hours before baking (see page 9).

The finished mug

This cheerful mug is easy to paint, and a matching mini teapot can be decorated in the same way. Here, I have painted the spout yellow and sponged the lid green.

Floral cup and saucer

These are sponged all over with yellow then the roses and leaves are painted in. The design is loosely outlined in black. Swirls are added to the centre of each flower. The areas between the flowers, the handle and edges are sponged in red.

Blue and white spotted mug

The rim of the mug is masked with masking tape and circular stickers are randomly applied around the mug. It is then sponged first with mid-blue, then with dark blue. Finally, the stickers and masking tape are removed.

Multicoloured striped and spotted mug

The mug is loosely painted with stripes of different colours. Dots and squiggles are then added.

Red and blue mottled cup

The cup is sponged using red and blue paints. When dry it is decorated with squiggles and dots using gold outliner.

Blue and white floral mug

This white mug is decorated with freestyle one-stroke painting.

Striped enamel mug

A 1cm (½in) flat brush is used to create wavy lines of different colours.

Cherry enamel mug

The lower edge of this mug is stamped with small red squares. The cherries are stamped around the middle, then the leaves and stems are painted in.

Waterbased porcelain paints are used on all these cups and mugs. Once baked, the paint is durable and items can be washed frequently.

Cat mug

Waterbased porcelain paints are used to create this mug. The cat design is transferred on to the front of the mug using carbon paper and the pattern provided. The design is outlined in black and allowed to dry. Masking tape is applied to the rim, the design is then filled in with paint and allowed to dry. The background is painted blue using random brushstrokes. The masking tape is removed and the rim and handle are painted yellow.

Pattern for the cat mug

Biscuit barrel

This cheerful biscuit barrel is decorated using the masking, sponging and stamping techniques. Durable waterbased porcelain paints are used as this item will need to be washed frequently. Three evenly spaced bands of masking tape are wrapped around the barrel and strips of tape are criss-crossed over the lid. The barrel and lid are sponged with bright colours and the masking tape is then removed. When dry, the uncoloured areas are sponged yellow. The barrel and lid are then stamped with a small heart-shaped stamp to complete the decoration. The lid knob is painted in a coordinating colour.

Grape tile

Transferring a design, masking, brushwork, outlining and highlighting

The techniques used in this project will give you a good opportunity to try out the paints and outliner. The grapes are coloured using the paint sparingly so that the texture of the brushstrokes is revealed. In contrast, plenty of paint is used to give a flat finish to the leaves and outer border. I have used a 15cm (6in) tile, but you can use any sized tile, and adjust the size of the pattern accordingly.

Students often ask me how to decorate tiles that are already glued into place on a wall and the answer is that it is not easy! If possible, tiles should be decorated flat before gluing into position. Certainly, for this project that is essential. However, if this is not possible, try masking around the tile to be decorated and then sponging paint on to form a base colour. The stamping or stencilling techniques shown elsewhere in this book are ideal for decorating vertical surfaces, as very little paint is applied and therefore runs are not a problem.

YOU WILL NEED
White ceramic tile
Waterbased porcelain paints: cream, blue, purple and green
Waterbased black outliner
Paintbrushes, Nos. 6 and 2
Piece of fine sponge
Cocktail stick
Masking tape
Tracing paper
Scissors
Fine black felt-tip pen
Ballpoint pen
Graphite paper
Palette

Pattern for the grape tile

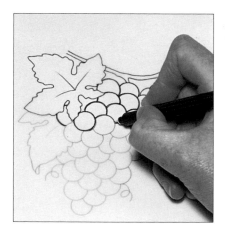

1. Trace the pattern provided using a fine black felt-tip pen, or photocopy it directly on to a piece of paper if you prefer.

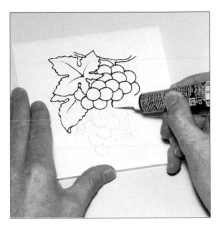

2. Cut the tracing paper approximately 0.5cm (¼in) smaller than the tile. Cut out a piece of graphite paper the same size as the tracing paper. Tape the top of the tracing paper to the tile; slip the graphite paper face down under the tracing paper and then tape the bottom to secure.

3. Trace over the outlined pattern with a ballpoint pen. Press firmly so that the design is transferred clearly on to the tile. Remove the tracing and graphite paper.

4. Use the black outliner to carefully outline the design. Work from the top of the tile, and gently squeeze the tube with an even pressure to produce a smooth, unbroken line. Do not outline the tendrils as these will be painted in at a later stage.

5. Mask around the edges and corners of the tile with masking tape. Press the edges of the tape down firmly, so that paint will not seep underneath.

6. Pour a little cream paint on to a palette. Sponge in a border around the outlined design. Remove the masking tape immediately, and allow to dry.

7. Paint in the grapes using blue paint and a No. 6 paintbrush. Try to get the brushstrokes working with the shape of the grapes. Do not leave to dry.

8. Dip a cocktail stick in water then use this to wipe out a dot of blue paint from the top right-hand corner of each grape to create highlights. Leave to dry.

9. Lightly shade the base of each grape using a little purple paint and a No. 6 brush. Allow to dry.

10. Paint the leaves and stem green using a No. 6 brush. Apply the paint generously when painting the leaves and try to avoid brushmarks.

11. Paint the small tendrils in green using a No. 2 brush.

12. Use a No. 6 paintbrush and purple paint to fill in the outer border. Apply the paint generously to avoid brush-strokes. Turn the tile around as you work. Allow to dry for twenty-four hours before baking (see page 9).

The finished tile

One or two of these vibrant tiles placed around your kitchen will add a touch of class to a plain wall. Alternatively, the finished tile could be framed, or used as a teapot stand.

Variation

You can paint your tile to match your own decor. Just by deepening the colour of the grapes and adding a dark blue border and an extra leaf, this tile looks quite different.

Use your imagination to create unusual tiles to decorate your home. Patterns for the designs can be found on pages 34–39).

Red apple tile

The apples and leaves are outlined in black then painted red and green. The highlights on the apples are wiped out with a cotton bud, and a blue background is painted in.

Colourful cat tile

The design is outlined using metallic copper outliner and filled in with bright, vibrant colours.

Fleur de lys tile

The blue background is sponged on, then the fleur de lys motif is stencilled in gold.

Sun tile

The design is outlined in blue using a paintbrush. The yellow areas are painted in and the red detail is added. Red and yellow are then sponged around the border.

Cat and mouse tile

The design is outlined in red outliner, then green and pink paint are sponged on to the cat. Blue paint is sponged on to the mice and the border is sponged in blue.

Fish tile

The fish is outlined in blue using simple strokes. Details are added and the fish is painted yellow. When dry, a thin wash of green paint is applied to the background.

Fruit tile

The design is outlined in black and filled in with strong Mediterranean colours.

Mermaid tile

The design is outlined with black outliner on to a mirror tile and painted with diluted glass paints.

Rose tile

The background is sponged yellow then the roses and leaves are painted in. The design is loosely outlined in black, using a brush. Swirls are added to the centre of each flower.

Pattern for the colourful cat tile featured on pages 32–33

Pattern for the fruit tile featured on pages 32–33

Pattern for the red apple tile featured on pages 32–33

Pattern for the mermaid tile featured on pages 32–33

*Pattern for the cat and mouse tile
featured on pages 32–33*

*Pattern for the fish tile featured
on pages 32–33*

Pattern for the rose tile featured on pages 32–33

Pattern for the sun tile featured on pages 32–33

Festive plate

OUTLINING AND PAINTING

I love Christmas, and what better way to decorate your home than with this colourful festive plate. Placed on a windowsill or lit from behind with a candle on a mantelpiece, you will be able to see clearly the wonderful vibrancy of the stained-glass colours. Remember to apply the paint generously to avoid brushmarks.

You can use a plate of any size for this project – simply adjust the pattern on a photocopier to fit. The outliner will take approximately half an hour to harden, so work carefully to avoid smudging. Mistakes can be removed with a cotton bud if the outliner is still wet; alternatively you can let it harden then carefully scrape it off with a knife.

YOU WILL NEED
Glass plate
Non-waterbased glass paints:
red, yellow, orange, green
and blue
Clear gloss glass painting
varnish
Black and gold glass painting
outliners
Masking tape
Soft paintbrush, No. 4
Palette

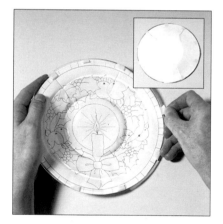

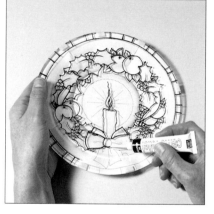

1. Photocopy the pattern opposite on to paper then cut it out. Place the design on the underside of the plate, then pleat the paper so that it lies flat against the glass. Tape into position with small pieces of masking tape. Do not put masking tape over any of the black lines of the pattern.

2. Outline the design (excluding the dots around the candle) using the black outliner. Gently squeeze the tube to produce a smooth, even line. Work from the top of the plate down, being careful not to smudge the outliner. Leave it to harden.

3. Use gold outliner to apply a circle of dots around the central candle flame. Allow to dry, then remove the pattern but do not throw it away. The remaining gold decoration will be added after the painting has been completed.

Pattern for the festive plate

41

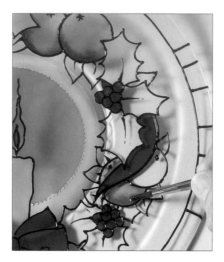

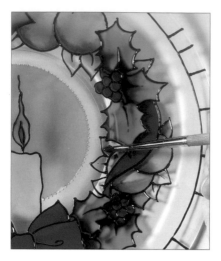

4. Mix one part yellow paint with four parts clear varnish and use this to paint the candle. Use a No. 4 paintbrush and apply the paint mixture generously to avoid brushmarks. Paint the centre of the flame red and the outer part orange. Paint yellow around the candle, up to the circle of gold dots.

5. Paint the berries, the ribbon and the bow with red. Carefully fill in the oranges using yellow. While the yellow paint is still wet, blend a little red and orange around the bottom of each orange to create shading.

6. Paint the holly leaves green. Mix a few drops of green with yellow and then use this olive colour to paint the leaves of the oranges.

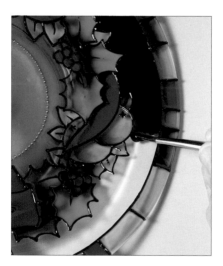

7. Paint the outer rim sections in alternating colours. Use all the colours on your palette. Allow to dry overnight.

8. Use orange paint to fill in the background area surrounding the central yellow circle. Paint the remaining border blue. Allow to dry overnight.

9. Place the pattern underneath the plate. Follow the design and use gold outliner to add dots around the flame. Finally, decorate with gold stars. Leave to dry for twenty-four hours.

The finished plate

This is a favourite design of mine, and it often inspires people to take up glass painting as a hobby!

Butterfly bowl

This octagonal glass bowl is decorated with non-waterbased glass paints and black outliner. A butterfly is transferred on to each side of the bowl using the pattern provided and carbon paper. The first butterfly is outlined and a line of outliner is piped around it. This is allowed to dry before moving on to the next butterfly. The bowl is worked in this way until all the sides are outlined. A row of vertical lines are added around the rim border and allowed to dry. One butterfly and background area is painted and left to dry before moving on to the next. This means that you are always working on a flat surface and the paints can dry flat. Finally, the rim border sections are decorated with different colours and, when dry, the base is painted.

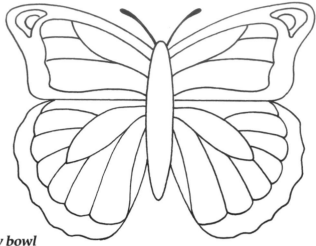

Pattern for the butterfly bowl

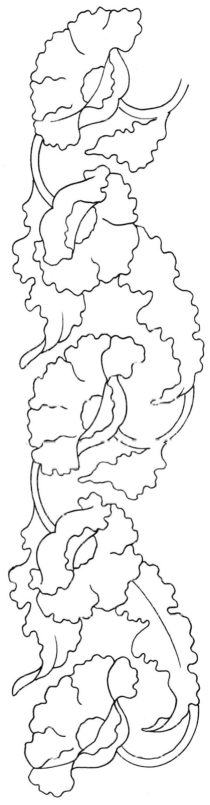

Pattern for the poppy bowl

Poppy bowl

This glass poppy bowl is outlined and painted on the outside using transparent waterbased porcelain paints. It is then sponged on the inside using metallic waterbased porcelain paints. The size of the pattern is increased so that it fits around the inside of the bowl. It is taped into position so that the design shows through the bowl. The design is outlined in black on the outside and allowed to dry. The poppy flowers, leaves and stems are then painted in. When dry, the inside of the bowl is sponged with copper paint.

45

Pink, pale blue and gold plate

Non-waterbased pink and gold ceramic paints are used to sponge the plate. The fine floral tracery is piped on using gold paint decanted into a plastic bottle fitted with a 0.5mm metal nozzle.

Eastern plate

Waterbased porcelain paints and outliners are used to create this plate. The design is transferred on to the plate using carbon paper and the pattern provided on page 49. It is then outlined with black outliner. The sections are painted in, working from the centre outwards. Gold outliner is used to add detail.

Stripy sunshine plate

The rim of this plate is decorated with stripes of bold colour using waterbased porcelain paints. When dry, dots and squiggles are added in contrasting colours and the centre is painted, leaving brushstrokes visible.

Embellished plate

The rim of this plate is masked before the centre is sponged with non-waterbased ceramic paints. While still wet, it is lightly oversponged with white spirit. The masking tape is removed and the plate allowed to dry before sponging the rim. When the rim is dry, glass droplets are glued into place then outlined in imitation lead outliner.

Mediterranean plate

Waterbased porcelain paints are used on this plate. The rim is painted loosely with fruits and leaves, then the centre is painted in a coordinating colour.

Folk art plate

This enamel plate is painted using non-waterbased ceramic paints to give a smooth flat finish. It is given two coats of the base colour. The design is drawn on to the plate using a white chinagraph pencil following the pattern provided on page 48. The flower petals and leaves are painted in bold colours using the one-stroke technique (see pages 50–51).

*Patterns for the folk art
plate featured on page 47*

Patterns for the Eastern
plate featured on page 47

49

Floral vase

FREEPAINTING

The loosely painted flowers and leaves in this project do not require great artistry, yet the overall effect is professional. This is a freepainting project. The pattern is provided as a guide to be used when painting the flowers and leaves. The arrows show the direction of the brushstrokes. Each flower, petal, stem and leaf is created with one stroke of the brush. The petals are pulled towards the centre of the flower, and the leaves are pulled towards the stem. Practice this one-stroke painting on paper before working on your vase so that you become familiar with the technique.

YOU WILL NEED

White ceramic vase
Waterbased porcelain paints:
pale pink, dark pink,
blue and gold
3 pieces of sponge
Paintbrushes, Nos. 4 and 6
Rigger paintbrush, No. 6
Palette

1. Sponge the entire vase with pale pink paint. Work as evenly as possible. Leave to dry.

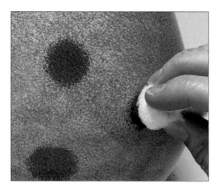

2. Randomly sponge assorted sized blue spots over the surface of the vase to form the flower heads. Allow to dry.

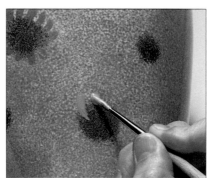

3. Use a No. 4 paintbrush and gold paint for the flower petals. Paint the top row first. Turn the vase and paint the bottom row of smaller petals. Leave to dry.

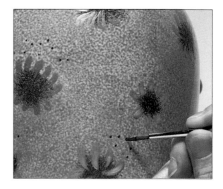

4. Add dots of gold and blue around each flower to represent pollen grains.

50

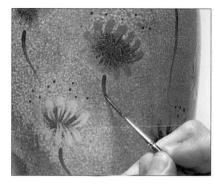

5. Paint in the stems using dark pink and a No. 6 rigger paintbrush.

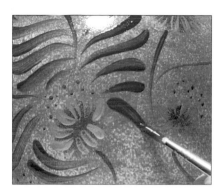

6. Use a No. 6 paintbrush and dark pink to paint the leaves. Fill in spaces with leaves to cover the whole vase.

7. Sponge the rim gold. Leave to dry for twenty-four hours before baking (see page 9).

The finished vase

This vase is painted using the simple one-stroke technique. You can vary the colour combinations to produce different effects (see pages 17 and 53).

Daisy vase

This glass vase is painted all over using non-waterbased glass paints, then it is left to dry. The daisy design is drawn on using a white chinagraph pencil. Non-waterbased ceramic paints are used to paint the leaves, flowers and pollen grains.

OPPOSITE

All these vases are painted using waterbased porcelain paints.

Floral vase

This vase is decorated using the basic one-stroke technique described on pages 50–51.

Relief vase

The basic colours are sponged on to the surface of this raised relief vase to give a mottled effect. When dry, gold highlights are sponged along the edges of the flower petals.

Abstract vase

This is probably one of the simplest pieces in the book. The vase is painted with random brushstrokes of alternating colour using a 1cm (½in) brush. The rim is then sponged with a coordinating colour.

Afternoon tea set

The items on this page are decorated using opaque waterbased porcelain paints and the freepainting one-stroke technique (see pages 50–51). Odd pieces can be painted with the same design to produce a matching set. The base coat is sponged on and allowed to dry before adding the one-stroke flowers and leaves. Rims and edges are sponged with gold.

OPPOSITE

Traditional coffee set

This coffee set is decorated using opaque waterbased porcelain paints. It is an extension of the freepainting one-stroke technique described on pages 50–51. The pieces are first sponged with a pastel colour and allowed to dry. They are then randomly sponged with small spots of paint to form a background for the floral decorations. The white flowers are painted in with a brush and the flower centres added. The leaves are painted using the one-stroke technique. When dry, the edges and rims are sponged with gold paint.

55

Flower pots

VERDIGRISING

This classic urn would grace any patio. The subtle verdigris finish and gold sponging highlight the relief pattern found on this terracotta pot. It is in fact a very easy technique to create with a few paints and pieces of sponge.

YOU WILL NEED

Terracotta pot
Waterbased acrylic paints: black, dark green, emerald green, light green and gold
3 pieces of sponge
No. 6 paintbrush
Palette

1. Use black paint and a No. 6 paintbrush to paint around the raised design and into the crevices.

2. Mix dark and emerald green paint with a little water, then sponge this all over the pot. Rub the paint into the crevices, allowing the black to show through slightly. Leave to dry.

3. Sponge light green paint on to the raised areas, and those which would weather naturally. The pot should now be completely covered in paint.

4. Use a sponge to dab a little gold paint over the light green areas, then rub it in to leave a subtle golden sheen.

The finished urn

Keep an eye open for pots with unusual shapes – new or old, they can easily be cleaned up and transformed with a few paints and this simple verdigrising technique.

MASKING, SPONGING AND STAMPING

This is a quick but very effective project. The simplicity of the white daisy stamped against a vivid blue background has transformed this ordinary plant pot. Sponging the rim is easier and quicker than painting it, and this creates a soft edge to the pot.

YOU WILL NEED

Terracotta pot

Waterbased acrylic paints: bright blue, white and orange

Masking tape

Paintbrush, No. 4

1cm (½in) flat brush

Daisy stamp

Sponge

Palette

The finished pot

This is a cheerful design and the pot can be used either indoors or out. The waterbased acrylic paints used in this and other projects give an excellent flat coverage and provide a weather-resistant finish.

1. Mask the top of the pot with masking tape. Press the edges of the masking tape down firmly. Do not mask the rim.

2. Sponge the rim with blue paint. Paint the main section of the pot using a 1cm (½in) flat brush. Remove the masking tape. Leave to dry.

3. Apply white paint to the daisy stamp. Stamp a daisy in the centre of the main blue section of the pot. Leave to dry.

4. Add lots of tiny dots of orange paint to the centre of the daisy using a No. 4 paintbrush. Leave to dry.

Red tulips add a splash of colour to any garden. With its yellow background and bold green leaves, this cheerful pot will brighten up even the dullest day.

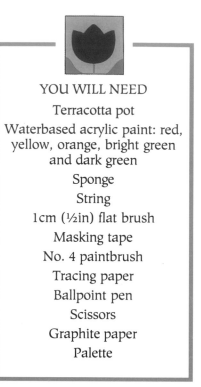

YOU WILL NEED

Terracotta pot

Waterbased acrylic paint: red, yellow, orange, bright green and dark green

Sponge

String

1cm (½in) flat brush

Masking tape

No. 4 paintbrush

Tracing paper

Ballpoint pen

Scissors

Graphite paper

Palette

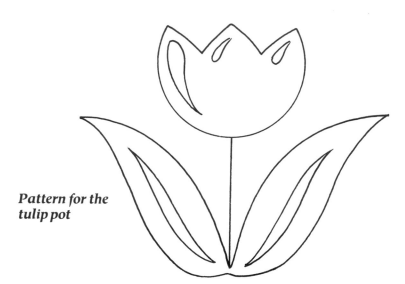

Pattern for the tulip pot

1. Mask the top of the pot with masking tape (see page 57). Sponge the rim red and paint the main section yellow. Leave to dry, then apply another coat of yellow to the main section. Allow to dry.

2. Sponge a band of bright green all the way around the base of the pot.

3. Divide the pot into quarters as shown. Mark the four points half way up the pot for the position of the tulips, using the string as a guide.

5. Trace the tulip pattern on to tracing paper. Cut it out and tape it on to the pot, positioning the middle of the tulip head over one of the four pencil marks. Slide graphite paper underneath. Trace over the outline with a ballpoint pen to transfer the design. Repeat until you have four tulips.

The finished pot

This simple design is painted on using the pattern provided, to create the tulip shapes. Try painting different flowers around your pot – sunflowers, poppies, daisies and roses can all look very effective, and you can vary your background colour to complement the design.

6. Paint in the flowers. Add orange dots between each tulip head. Allow to dry, then add stripes of shading to the tulip heads and leaves.

PAGES 60–61

Selection of terracotta pots

Group your decorated pots together to create a colourful display in your garden. Limit your colour palette for a more coordinated look. The main colours used to decorate these pots are red, yellow, blue and green. Simple spots and stripes are easy to paint but they look very effective. A border of strawberries painted around the rim of a larger pot adds a spot of colour whilst you are waiting for those early flowers to bloom. An overall design of fruit or flowers will take a little more time to do but is well worth the effort. Get out those paints and pots and have a go!

Perfume bottle

PAINTING AND EMBELLISHING

The addition of beads and metallic outliner to a painted glass bottle really does transform it. Use rich, vibrant colours and choose beads to match or complement the background colours. I have used turquoise and clear glass beads for this bottle, but you could use more strongly contrasting colours if you wish. Group a few decorated bottles together on a windowsill to create a stunning effect and reveal the beauty of these paints.

YOU WILL NEED

Small flat-sided glass bottle with cork

Silver glass painting outliner

Small beads

Non-waterbased glass paints: turquoise

Tracing paper

Ballpoint pen

Scissors

Carbon paper

Masking tape

Cocktail stick

Paintbrush, No. 4

Pattern for the perfume bottle

1. Trace the heart pattern on to tracing paper. Cut it out and tape it on to the bottle. Slide carbon paper underneath. Trace over the outline with a ballpoint pen to transfer the design then remove the masking tape, tracing and carbon paper.

2. Outline the heart with silver outliner. Fill in the heart with the outliner, then use the nozzle to smooth out the paste.

3. Immediately lie the bottle on a plate. Sprinkle the heart with beads, then arrange them carefully using a cocktail stick. Fill in any spaces using beads from the plate, picked up on the cocktail stick. Leave the outliner to harden.

4. Use the silver outliner to add a diamond shape to one of the four corners. Decorate with beads (see step 3). Repeat on the other three corners. Leave the outliner to harden.

5. Hold the neck of the bottle then paint the bottle turquoise, starting at the bottom. Carefully paint around the beaded sections. When you get near the top, stand the bottle up to paint the neck. Allow to dry.

6. Use the outliner to add dots in a line between each beaded diamond section and towards the neck of the bottle. Add a row of dots down each edge of the bottle. Allow to dry.

7. Paint the sides of the cork with silver outliner using a No. 4 brush. Leave to dry. Apply a thick layer of outliner directly from the tube to the top of the cork. Decorate immediately with beads. Allow to dry.

The finished bottle
Sparkling glass beads look stunning against the rich turquoise of this bottle.

Pages 64–65

Selection of perfume bottles
Empty miniature bottles provide unusual shapes to decorate. Designs can become very intricate when working on such a small scale. Remember to paint the stoppers to match the bottles.

The bottles on page 64 are decorated with glass paints and metallic outliners. The bottles on page 65 are decorated using waterbased porcelain paints and outliners.

OPPOSITE

Eastern bottle

This metal bottle is decorated using waterbased porcelain paints and outliners. The patterns are transferred on to the surface using carbon paper. The designs are outlined in black outliner and left to dry. The bottle is painted and, when dry, detailing is added using gold outliner. The cork is removed before baking.

Patterns for the Eastern bottle

Biscuit tin

SPONGING, STAMPING, FREEPAINTING AND WIPING OUT

This biscuit tin started life as a coffee container. I am an inveterate hoarder and cannot bear to throw anything away. I love the feeling of satisfaction when creating something from nothing. The sponging, stamping and freepainting techniques are all combined in this project. The tin illustrated here is 20cm (8in) tall and 15cm (6in) in diameter, but you can adapt the design to fit any sized tin.

The finished tin
Simple techniques are used to create this colourful container. You can vary the colour scheme to match the decor of your own home.

YOU WILL NEED

Metal tin

Waterbased porcelain paints: white, deep blue, scarlet and olive green

Piece of fine sponge

Fine grade sandpaper

Lighter fuel or methylated spirit

Soft cloth

Cotton bud

Paintbrush, No. 6

Rigger brush, No. 6

Small circular stamp and small square stamp

Palette

1. Sand the tin to remove any rough spots or irregularities. Wipe down the tin with a soft cloth and lighter fuel or methylated spirit.

2. Sponge the tin using a fine sponge and white paint. Allow to dry thoroughly then repeat to create a good opaque base on which to work. Allow to dry.

3. Stamp on two rows of blue squares (see page 19) at the top and bottom of the tin to create a gingham border.

4. Stamp a red cherry on to the tin. Overstamp it, then use a damp cotton bud to remove a small area of paint and create a highlight. Repeat until the tin is covered in highlighted cherries. Allow to dry.

5. Use green paint and a No. 6 rigger brush to paint in the stems. Use green paint and a No. 6 paintbrush for the leaves. Add as many leaves as you like, to fill in any spaces. Leave to dry for twenty-four hours before baking (see page 9.)

Watering can

Non-waterbased ceramic paints are used on this project. The body of the can is painted blue and, when dry, it is decorated with simple one-stroke flowers in alternate colours. A striped spout and handle add the finishing touch to this zany container.

Green folk art tin

The base colour and red band around the rim are painted using non-waterbased ceramic paints. When dry, the folk art design is drawn on using a white chinagraph pencil. The flowers and leaves are painted in using the one-stroke technique (see pages 50–51).

Small lilac floral tin

This can is sponged with waterbased porcelain paints and left to dry. Simple white daisies are painted and small dots of colour are added in between the flowers.

RIGHT

Daisy bucket

This bucket is painted using green non-waterbased ceramic paint. When completely dry, strips of masking tape are used to create the blue and white vertical stripes and the blue line around the base. White daisies are stamped around the bottom section of the bucket and the centre of each daisy and the handle of the bucket are painted orange.

Shell bowl

DRIBBLING AND STENCILLING

This project introduces you to the dribbling technique, which can be used with all non-waterbased ceramic and glass paints. It makes an interesting decorative finish on its own, or it can be used as a background for stencilling or stamping, for example. You should use a clean piece of sponge for each colour you apply; this will maintain the vibrancy of the paints. This shell bowl is great fun to decorate, but the dribbling technique can be surprisingly messy, so protect your clothes and cover your work surface with layers of newspaper.

YOU WILL NEED

Ceramic bowl

Non-waterbased ceramic paints: royal blue, petrol blue, turquoise, deep pink and gold

6 pieces of sponge

White spirit

Stencil paper

Pencil

Saucer

Masking tape

Thick card

Scalpel or craft knife

Absorbent paper

Small tin, slightly smaller than the base of the bowl

Newspaper

Palette

Pattern for the shell bowl stencil

The finished bowl
Striking marine colours contrast brilliantly with this gold shell motif. Filled with fragrant soaps, this bowl would enhance any bathroom.

1. Pour a small pool of each colour (excluding gold) on to your palette. Sponge the entire bowl with random spots of paint using a clean piece of sponge for each colour.

2. Place the wet bowl on top of a small tin to raise it from your work surface. Pour some white spirit into a saucer, then use this to lightly sponge the surface of the bowl. Start at the rim and work down, allowing the white spirit to run.

3. Leave the bowl in position on the tin. Wipe the base with absorbent paper to remove any drips of paint. Leave to dry for twenty-four hours.

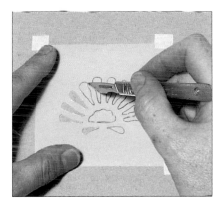

4. Trace the shell pattern opposite on to stencil paper. Tape the stencil paper on to a piece of thick card, then cut out the sections of the design using a scalpel or craft knife. Remove the masking tape.

5. Attach the stencil to the top of the bowl using masking tape. Lightly sponge over it with gold paint. Repeat, continuing the design all around the top of the bowl. Leave to dry.

6. Sponge the rim with gold paint. Leave to dry.

Fleur de lys bowl

Non-waterbased glass paints are used to sponge this glass bowl using the technique described on pages 72–73. Gold non-waterbased ceramic paints are used to stencil four fleur de lys motifs around the bowl (see the pattern on page 77). Tulip heads are stamped upside down between the motifs and the rim is then sponged gold.

Star bowl

This bowl is an old copper one I bought very cheaply from a junk shop. It is decorated using the dribbling technique and non-waterbased ceramic paints. The original copper shows through the paint here and there to give an interesting effect. Stencilled stars add the finishing touch (see page 77).

Leaf bowl

This uses the same technique as the star and fleur de lys bowls, but white is added to the paint to create pastel shades (see page 77 for the pattern).

Fish bowl

Blue and green non-waterbased ceramic paints are used with the dribbling technique (see pages 72–73) to create the watery-looking background on this bowl. This is allowed to dry for twenty-four hours before the designs are transferred on to the side of the bowl using carbon paper and the patterns provided. The fish are painted and left to dry. The detailing on the fins and scales is then added using gold paint decanted into a plastic bottle fitted with a 0.5mm metal nozzle. Finally, the rim is sponged with gold paint.

Pattern for the fleur de lys bowl featured on page 74

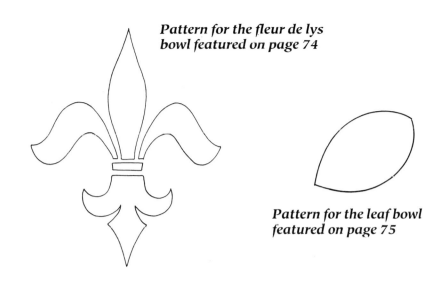

Pattern for the leaf bowl featured on page 75

Pattern for the star bowl featured on page 75

Patterns for the fish bowl opposite

Index

A

absorbent paper 8, 12, 13, 73
acetate 12

B

baking 9, 14
ballpoint pen 12, 13, 59, 62
beads 12, 17, 20, 62, 63
biscuit barrel 27
biscuit tin 68–69
blanks 12, 13, 16
blending 21
bottle
  Eastern 66–67
  green wine 1, 4
  metal 66, 67
  perfume 62–63, 64–65
  small green 1, 4
bowl
  butterfly 1, 44
  fish 76
  fleur de lys 74
  leaf 75
  poppy 45
  shell 72–73
  star 75
brushes 12, 13
brushstrokes 9, 10, 14, 15,
  18, 21, 26, 28, 29, 50, 53
bucket, daisy 7, 71

C

carbon paper 12, 13, 26, 47,
  62, 67, 76
ceramicware 8, 12, 13, 16
chinagraph pencil 47, 52, 71
cocktail stick 8, 12, 13, 30, 62
coffee set 54, 55
cooling rack 12, 13
cotton bud 8, 12, 13, 19, 33,
  40, 69
craft knife 12, 73
cup see also mug
  floral 24

D

decanter, glass 1, 4
dribbling 4, 10, 12, 17, 20, 21,
  72–73, 74, 75, 76

E

embellishing 11, 17, 20

F

felt-tip pen 12, 13
flower pot see pot
freepainting 17, 50–51, 55,
  68–69

G

glassware 8, 12, 13, 16
goblet, metal 17
graphite paper 12, 13, 29, 59

L

lighter fuel 12, 13, 16, 69

M

masking 4, 12, 19, 22, 24, 27,
  28, 29, 47, 57, 58
masking tape 12, 13, 26, 40, 71,
  73
metalware 12, 13, 16
methylated spirit 12, 16, 69
mug see also cup
  blue and white floral 24
  blue and white spotted 24
  cat 6, 26
  cherry enamel 24–25
  multicoloured striped and
    spotted 24–25
  red and blue mottled 24
  striped enamel 24–25
  tulip 22–23

O

one-stroke technique 14, 18,
  24, 4, 47, 50–51, 52, 55, 71
opaque finish 21
outliner 4, 10, 11, 14, 15,
  20, 28, 29,
  40, 44, 47, 62, 63
outlining 17, 19, 20, 24, 26,
  29, 33, 40, 44, 45, 47, 67

I hope you have enjoyed this
book as much as I have
enjoyed creating it.